W9-BAT-449

COUGARS

Cindy Rodriguez

EYE to EYE
with Endangered Species

ROURKE PUBLISHING
Vero Beach, Florida 32964

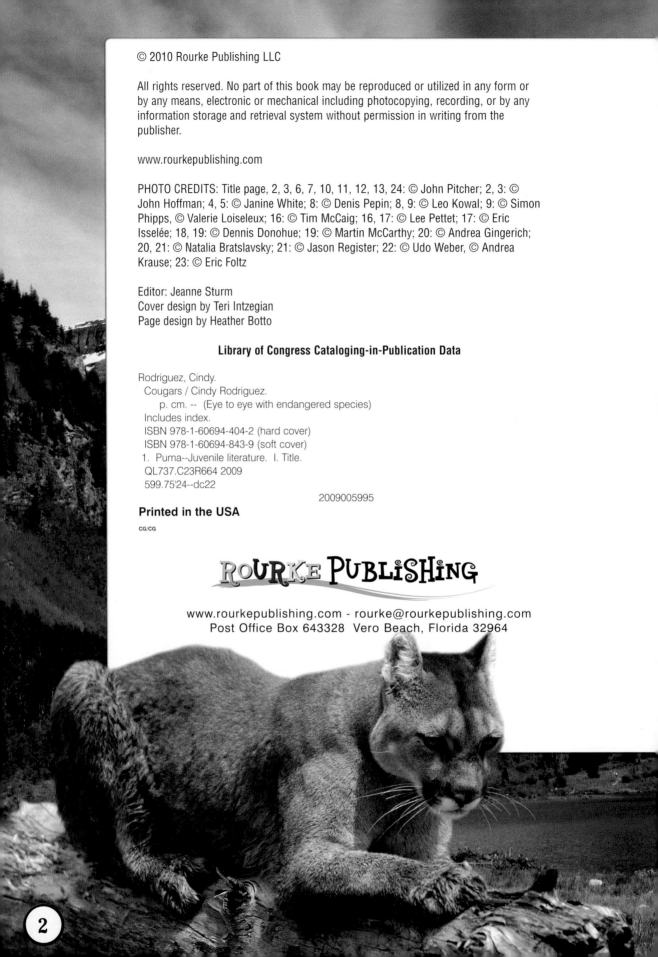

www.rourkepublishing.com

PHOTO CREDITS: Title page, 2, 3, 6, 7, 10, 11, 12, 13, 24: © John Pitcher; 2, 3: © John Hoffman; 4, 5: © Janine White; 8: © Denis Pepin; 8, 9: © Leo Kowal; 9: © Simon Phipps, © Valerie Loiseleux; 16: © Tim McCaig; 16, 17: © Lee Pettet; 17: © Eric Isselée; 18, 19: © Dennis Donohue; 19: © Martin McCarthy; 20: © Andrea Gingerich; 20, 21: © Natalia Bratslavsky; 21: © Jason Register; 22: © Udo Weber, © Andrea Krause; 23: © Eric Foltz

Editor: Jeanne Sturm
Cover design by Teri Intzegian
Page design by Heather Botto

Library of Congress Cataloging-in-Publication Data

Rodriguez, Cindy.
  Cougars / Cindy Rodriguez.
      p. cm. -- (Eye to eye with endangered species)
  Includes index.
  ISBN 978-1-60694-404-2 (hard cover)
  ISBN 978-1-60694-843-9 (soft cover)
  1. Puma--Juvenile literature. I. Title.
  QL737.C23R664 2009
  599.75'24--dc22
                                              2009005995

Printed in the USA

CG/CG

ROURKE PUBLISHING

www.rourkepublishing.com - rourke@rourkepublishing.com
Post Office Box 643328 Vero Beach, Florida 32964

Table of Contents

Puma, mountain lion, panther, ghost cat, and catamount are all names for the mysterious cougar. Some of the over twenty **endangered** subspecies now fight to take back their **habitats**.

This animal is the second largest cat. Only the jaguar is bigger. The cougar's long, slender body is red-brown or gray-brown with a round head and ears that stand tall to listen for its next meal. These special animals measure 6 to 8 feet (1.8 to 2.4 meters) long, and weigh, on average, about 150 pounds (68 kilograms).

Adult cougars hunt large animals such as deer, elk, and moose, while younger cougars prey on coyotes, raccoons, and small rodents.

A Population at Risk

Long ago, the cougar was spread far and wide in North America. They roamed coastal marshes, mountains, and forests. Over time, settlers built homes and farms in areas where the animals roamed. Fearing the cougars would eat their livestock; farmers killed them. Now, most of the eastern cougars are **extinct.**

Cougars make their dens in caves on mountain cliffs. In less mountainous areas, they find shelter in the space under fallen trees or large roots.

Depending on where the cougar lives, it might have a different name. South American cougars are often called pumas, while Florida cougars are often called panthers.

The Cougar's Prey

The white-tailed deer is the cougar's preferred meal. Cougars can eat one deer a week. The drastic decrease in the population of the white-tailed deer caused much of the cougar's disappearance in the eastern United States.

White-Tailed Deer

A cougar can eat up to 20 pounds (9 kilograms) of deer at a time. When full, it will bury the carcass to save it for another day.

Elk

Beaver

Hare

Fun Fact

Watch out! If you come across a deer that appears to have been a meal for a cougar, stay away. Cougars are known to cover the remains of a kill and return to eat parts of it over several days.

Camouflage

The spotted fur on the cougar's ears and tail help him stay camouflaged, or hidden, while he waits to **ambush** his prey. Cougars do not chase their meals but rather **stalk** them from behind. These lone hunters stay hidden until they are ready to attack by pouncing on their prey. They might also climb trees and leap far distances for their food. Their long tails help them balance and thrust forward. As forests are cut down and housing developments appear, the cougars lose areas in which to hide to catch their dinner.

Fun Fact

Ghost cat *is a name given to the cougar because it quietly moves about the forest as it hunts for its next meal.*

A cougar from the North Dakota Badlands will often use steep canyons, rocks, and boulders to remain hidden while hunting.

Cougar Kittens

Cougars are ready to have their babies by the time they are 2 years old. A cougar has up to three kittens every two or three years. The mother and kittens make up the cougar family.

These young animals stay with their mother until they are about a year old, when they can go out on their own. She teaches them how to live in the wild. Often, mothers are killed by hunters and the babies then struggle to survive. The father cougar lives and hunts alone.

The mother cougar feeds her kitten milk for three months. Like a domestic cat, the young cougar is born with its eyes closed. It opens its eyes when it is 8 to 9 days old.

Cougar Habitats

Established Cougar Habitats

North
America

South
America

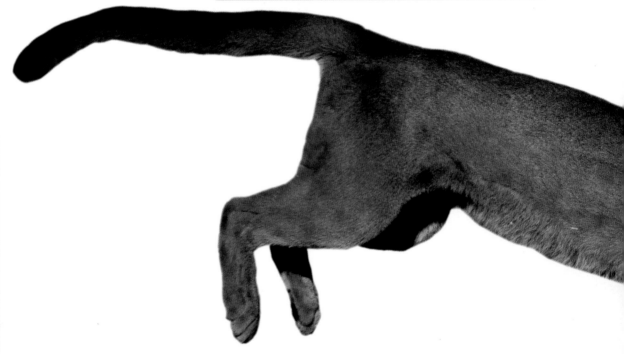

Using its powerful hind legs, the cougar can jump up an 18-foot (6-meter) cliff or make a forward leap up to 30 feet (9 meters) long. This skill helps the animal hunt along mountain rocks.

Cougars need large areas of land to survive. These animals are **territorial**, staying in the one area they defend and protect. **Deforestation** has limited their habitats and that of their prey. Their past homelands are now split up for a variety of land uses that disrupt the expansive area cougars require to thrive.

Cougar Enemies

Cougars have no natural enemies. People are the cougar's only **predator**. Humans feared the cougar would hurt their animals and even, possibly, themselves. Their solution was unlimited hunting of this misunderstood animal. White-tailed deer were also relentlessly hunted to near extinction, taking away the cougar's main source of food. Habitat disturbances, such as housing developments, have also caused the downfall of the eastern cougar.

**WARNING
MOUNTAIN LION
COUNTRY**

A RISK

MOUNTAIN LIONS MAY BE PRESENT AND ARE UNPREDICTABLE. BE CAUTIOUS. THEY HAVE BEEN KNOWN TO ATTACK WITHOUT WARNING. YOUR SAFETY CANNOT BE GUARANTEED. YOU ARE ADVISED TO STAY ALERT TO POTENTIAL DANGERS.

REPORT ALL MOUNTAIN LION SIGHTINGS TO THE PARK OFFICE.

Cougars can live up to twenty years in the wild and even longer in captivity.

Help Is On the Way!

The Endangered Species Act says it is illegal to hunt an endangered species, although in some places cougars can still be hunted if strict laws and guidelines are followed.

Cougars are very territorial. A male cougar makes its home on about 100 square miles (259 square kilometers) of land.

Fortunately, the western United States has been able to support the cougar. The large amounts of open land west of the Mississippi River help the cougar survive. **Biologists** use information learned about the cougars living in the west to establish and support cougars in the eastern United States.

Advanced DNA testing and more evidence from experts prove that cougars are attempting to survive in the East. Some believe that these are not **native** cougars. They could be pets that were released or cougars who have traveled east from their original habitat. In either case, many want to protect this endangered species.

ologists use radio
acking devices to monitor
ildlife movement.

Cougars in the Eastern Half of the United States

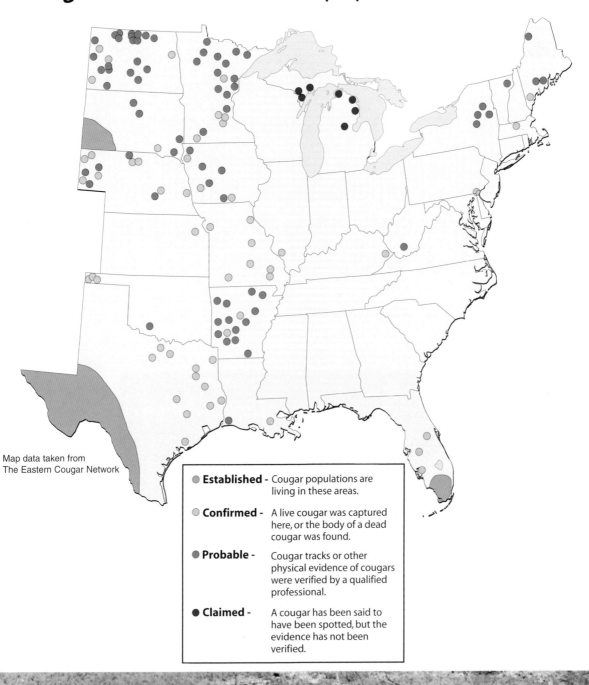

Map data taken from
The Eastern Cougar Network

Established - Cougar populations are living in these areas.

Confirmed - A live cougar was captured here, or the body of a dead cougar was found.

Probable - Cougar tracks or other physical evidence of cougars were verified by a qualified professional.

Claimed - A cougar has been said to have been spotted, but the evidence has not been verified.

The populations still breeding are the western mountain lions and the endangered Florida panther. Although the Florida panther is federally protected, the western cougar's population is more secure. Current research works toward a peaceful coexistence between humans and these mammals as they return to their original habitats.

Florida Panther

Glossary

ambush (AM-bush): to hide and then attack your prey

biologists (bye-OL-uh-jists): scientists who study living things

deforestation (dee-FOR-is-tay-shuhn): the removal or cutting down of trees in a forest

endangered (en-DAYN-jurd): when a species of plant or animal is in danger of becoming extinct

extinct (ek-STINGKT): when a species of plant or animal dies out

habitats (HAB-uh-tats): the natural places where animals live

native (NAY-tiv): a person, animal, or plant that is originally from a certain place

predator (PRED-uh-tur): an animal that hunts other animals

stalk (STAWK): to hunt an animal in a quiet, secret way

territorial (TER-uh-tor-ee-uhl): an animal's tendency to defend the area where it lives

Index

Websites to Visit

www.cougarfund.org/
www.cougarnet.org/
www.cougarfund.org/morereferences.php

About the Author

Cindy Rodriguez has been teaching first graders how to read for more than 20 years. She loves using nonfiction books to involve her students in real world situations that make their reading exciting. "Caretakers of the Earth" is the motto for Cindy's school in Vero Beach, Florida, so investigating endangered species is one of her passions. She enjoys long distance running and traveling to explore new places with her two teenage daughters.